Early to Later Elementary ♦ 1 Piano, 4 Hands

# DAY AT THE FAIR

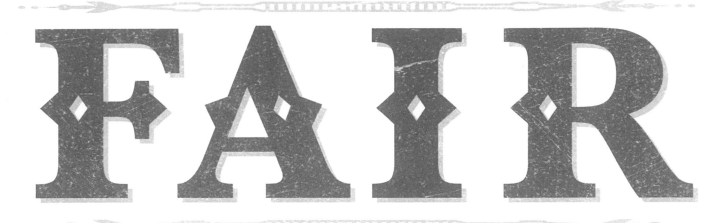

## by Naoko Ikeda

ISBN 978-1-5400-8227-5

WILLIS MUSIC

EXCLUSIVELY DISTRIBUTED BY

HAL•LEONARD®

World headquarters, contact:
**Hal Leonard**
7777 West Bluemound Road
Milwaukee, WI 53213
Email: info@halleonard.com

In Europe, contact:
**Hal Leonard Europe Limited**
1 Red Place
London, W1K 6PL
Email: info@halleonardeurope.com

In Australia, contact:
**Hal Leonard Australia Pty. Ltd.**
4 Lentara Court
Cheltenham, Victoria, 3192 Australia
Email: info@halleonard.com.au

# Hello there! Welcome to the fairgrounds.

As you approach, you see big, colorful tents arranged neatly in several rows. There's also a dazzling carousel, an enormous ferris wheel, and an ice cream stand with 100 different flavors.

And there's SO much music! Time to explore.

## The Pegasus on the Carousel

Let's get in line and take a ride on the carousel. Choose the strong Pegasus with his head held high and imagine flying up in the sky on his huge wings.

## The Jokey Juggler

You turn a corner and see a clown making funny faces as he juggles pins in the air. But how does he catch all those pins – two is easy, three is a little harder, but seven? Wow. And look carefully – in the air they start to sparkle!

## Ice Cream Time

Time for a treat. What's your favorite ice cream flavor? Chocolate, mint chip, black cherry? Whatever it is, let's each buy a scoop, sit down, and take a break. Look up – you'll see many kites flying in the clear blue sky.

## Story of a Star

We enter one of the little tents and watch a puppet play! It's telling the story of a poor orphan girl who practices hard every night. She grows up to be a famous opera singer with the most beautiful voice in the world.

### Bumper Car Joy

It's time for a bumper car race – get in your car and let's go! Enjoy the sounds of horns and laughter, and be careful as you drive. Beep beep!

### Little Flamenco Dancer

A performance is about to begin. A handsome guitarist sings and strums confidently as a lady with a red rose behind her right ear starts to dance. Clap your hands along with everyone else and enjoy the steady rhythms!

### Farewell to the Fair

The sun has set and this wonderful day has come to an end. As everyone begins walking to the exit, soft chimes play in the distance. So long, farewell, *ciao, jah-neh*, and we'll see you again next year. Let's go home.

# CONTENTS

# The Pegasus on the Carousel

SECONDO

Naoko Ikeda

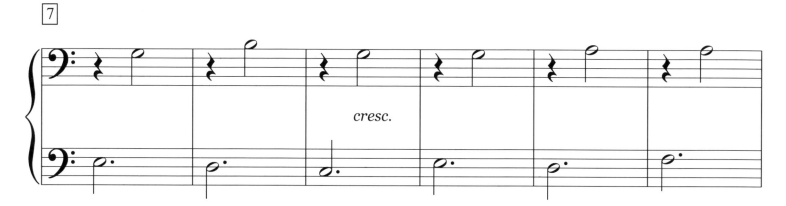

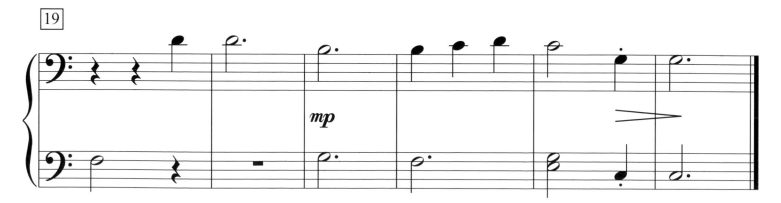

# The Pegasus on the Carousel

PRIMO

Naoko Ikeda

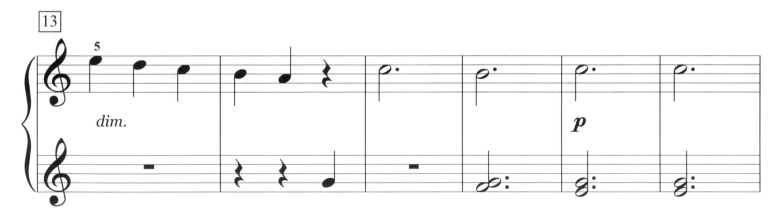

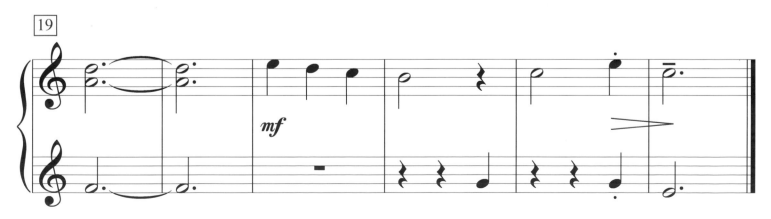

# The Jokey Juggler

### SECONDO

Naoko Ikeda

**With charm**

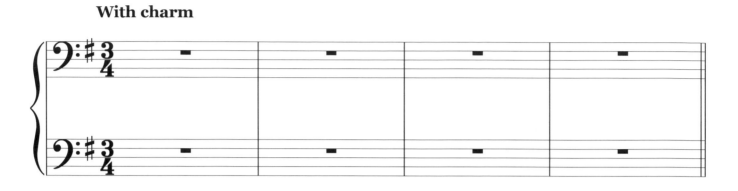

# The Jokey Juggler

PRIMO

Naoko Ikeda

**With charm**
*Play both hands one octave higher than written*

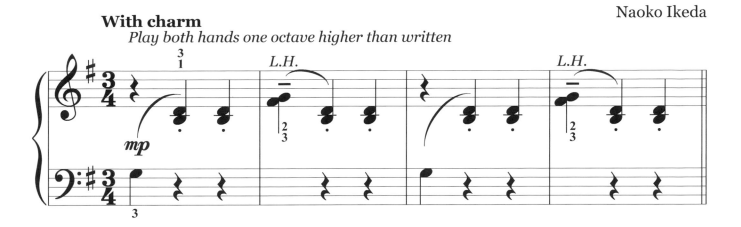

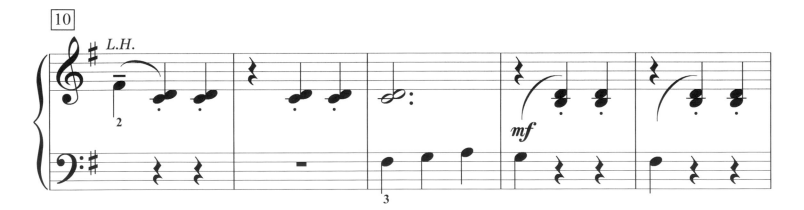

# Ice Cream Time

## SECONDO

Naoko Ikeda

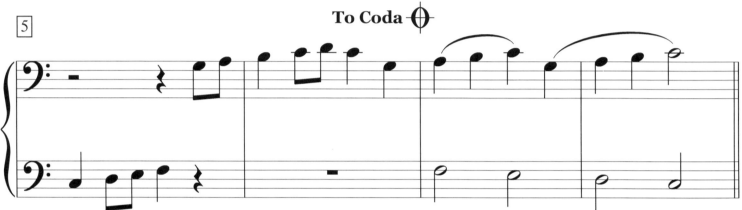

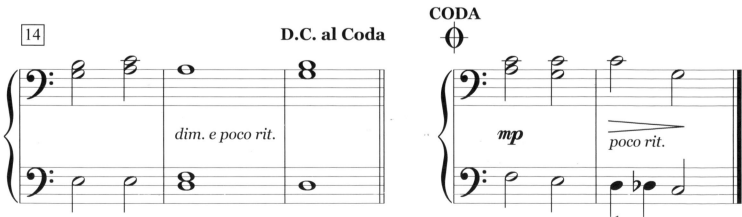

# Ice Cream Time

PRIMO

Naoko Ikeda

**Moderato, relaxed**

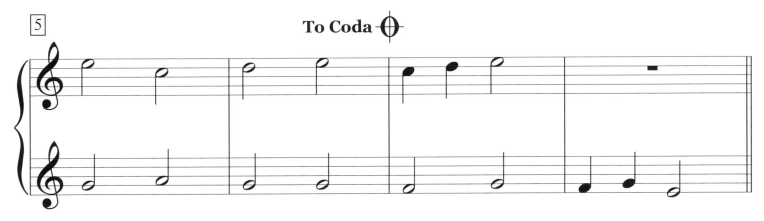

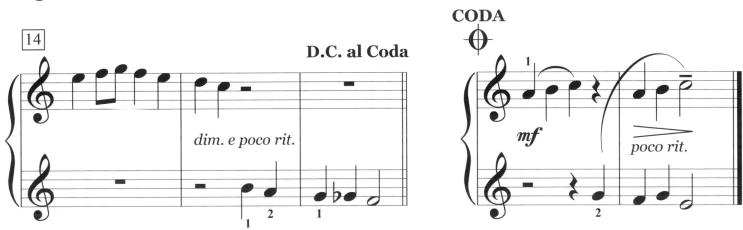

# Story of a Star

SECONDO

Naoko Ikeda

**Andantino cantabile**

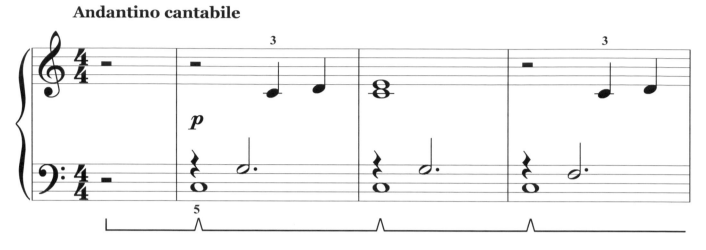

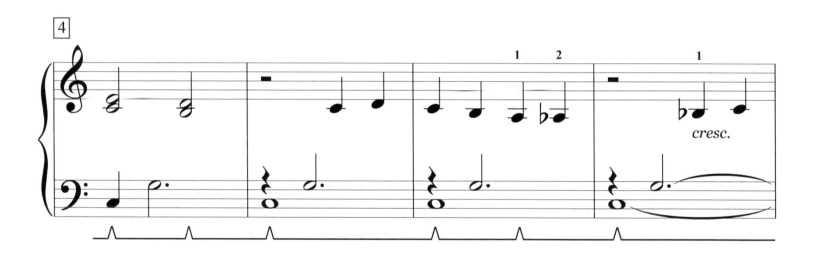

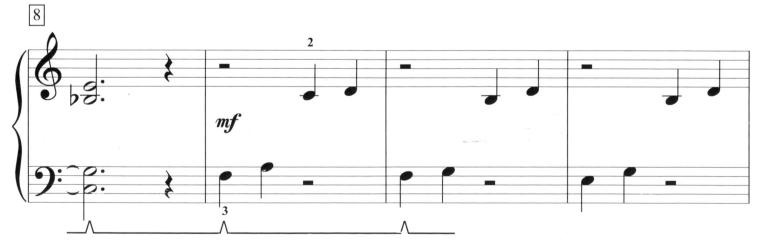

# Story of a Star

PRIMO

Naoko Ikeda

### Andantino cantabile
*Play both hands one octave higher than written*

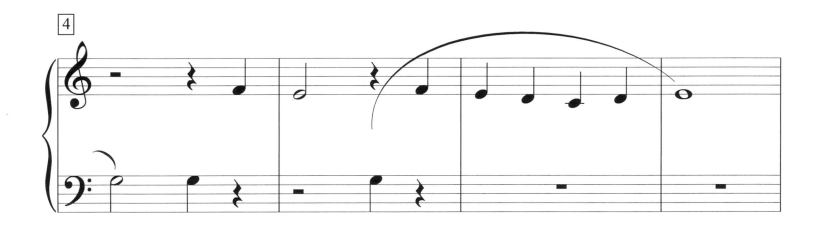

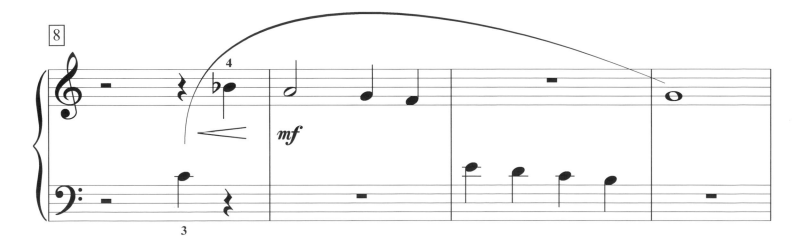

SECONDO

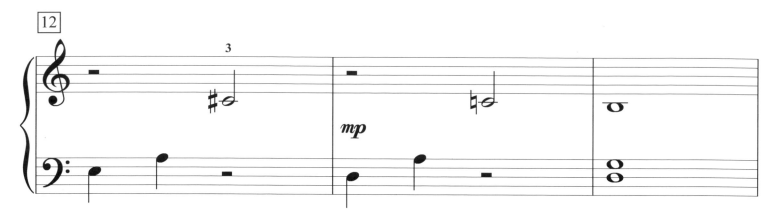

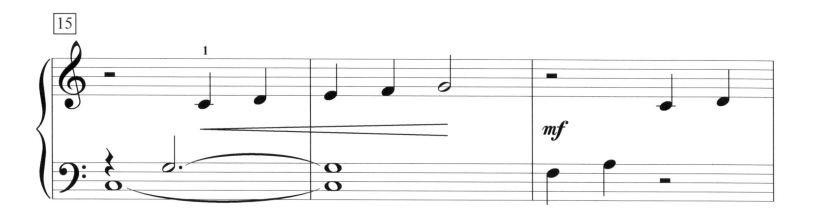

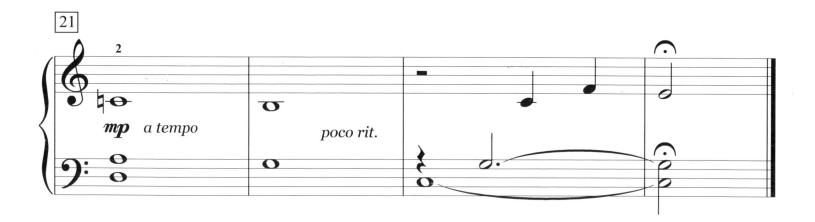

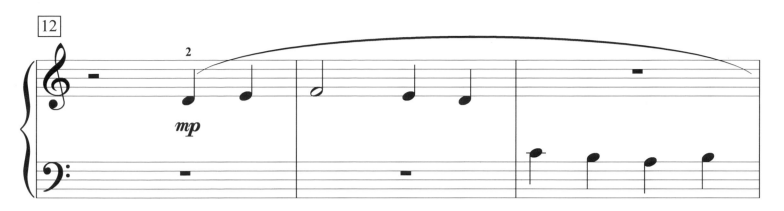

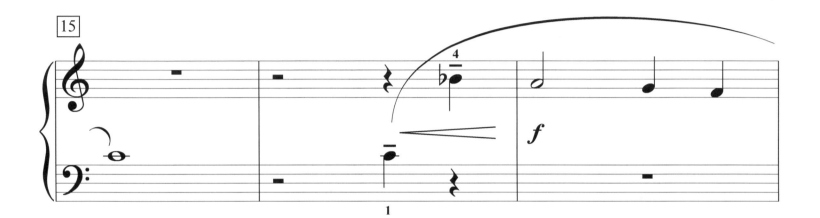

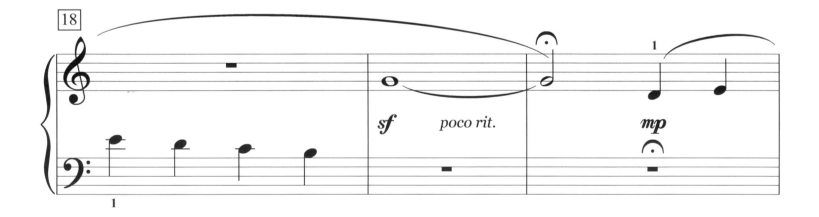

# Bumper Car Joy

SECONDO

Naoko Ikeda

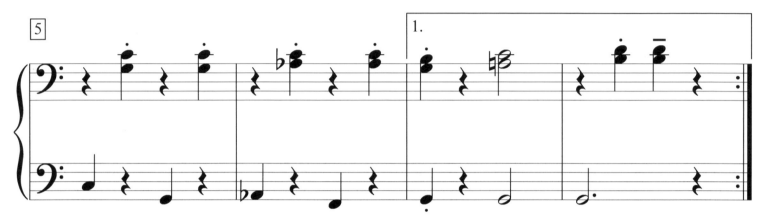

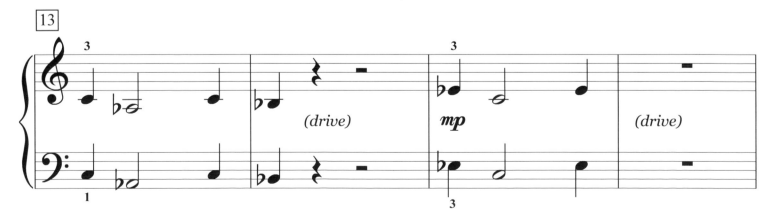

# Bumper Car Joy

PRIMO

Naoko Ikeda

* *Play with open palms!*

SECONDO

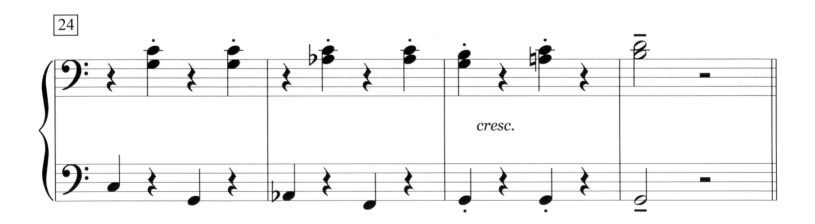

PRIMO

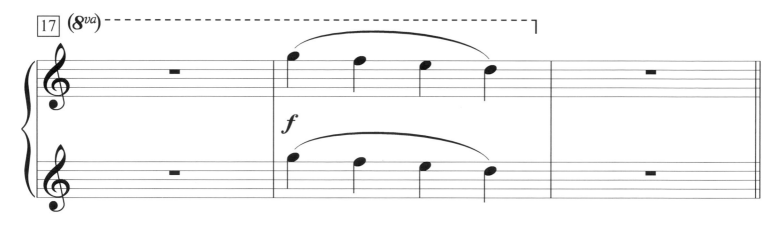

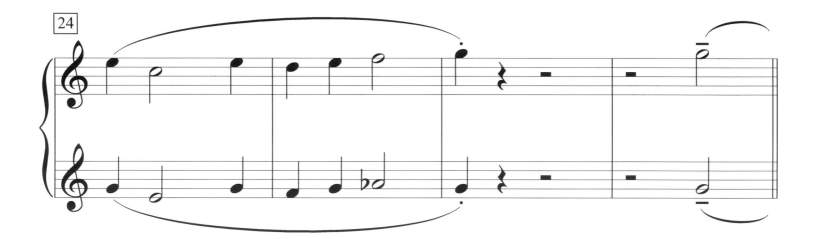

Beep, beep!

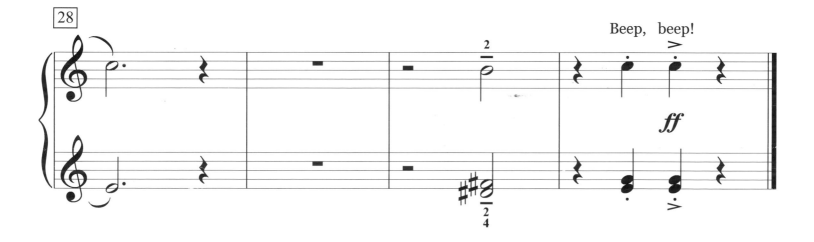

# Little Flamenco Dancer

## SECONDO

Naoko Ikeda

**Allegretto con moto**

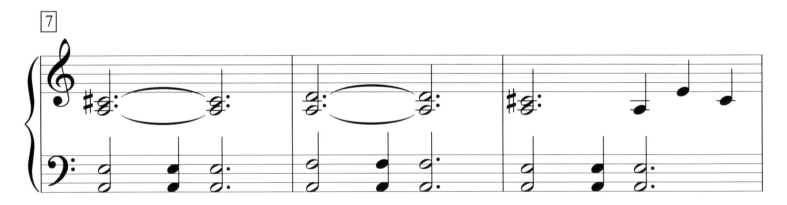

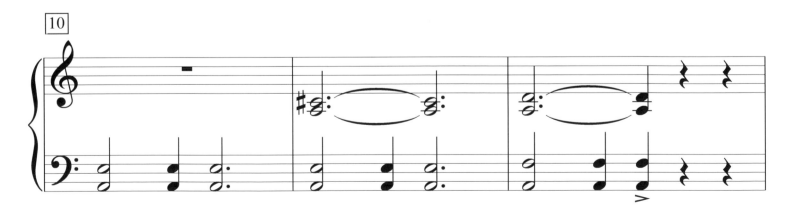

# Little Flamenco Dancer

PRIMO

Naoko Ikeda

**Allegretto con moto**

*R.H. one octave higher than written*

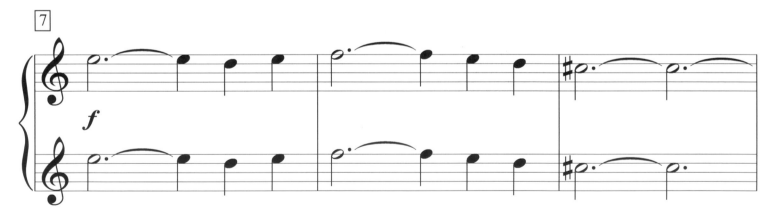

SECONDO

**Very freely**

*Play both hands one octave lower*

**Tempo I**

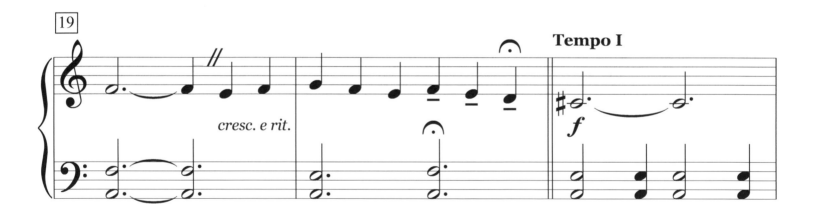

*Keep L.H. one octave lower*

# Farewell to the Fair

SECONDO

Naoko Ikeda

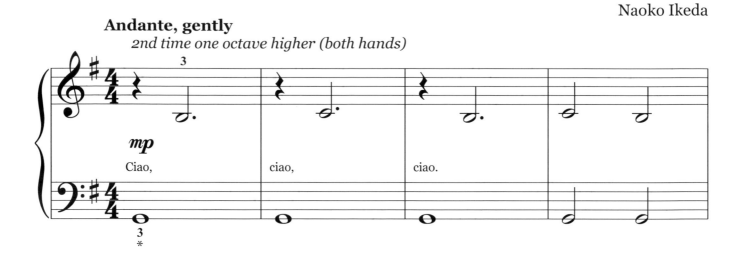

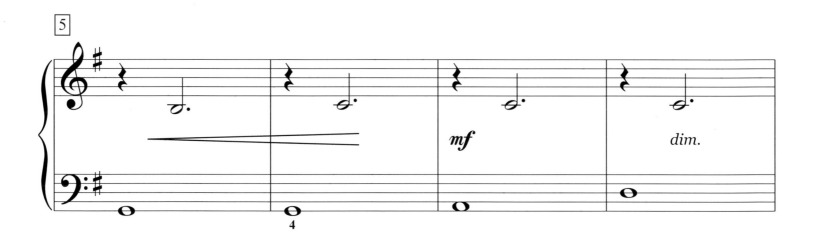

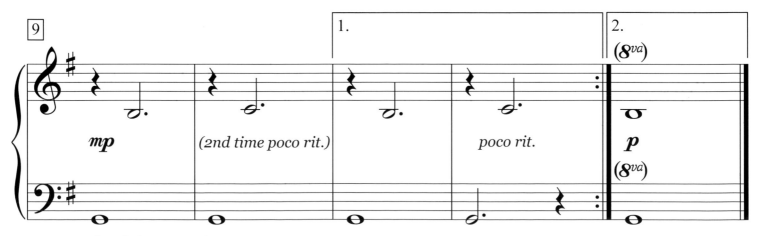

* Optional pedal on each downbeat.

# Farewell to the Fair

PRIMO

Naoko Ikeda

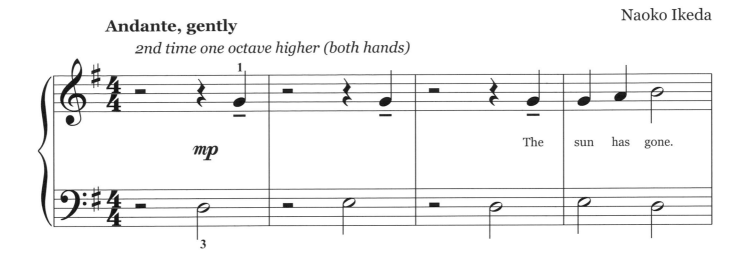

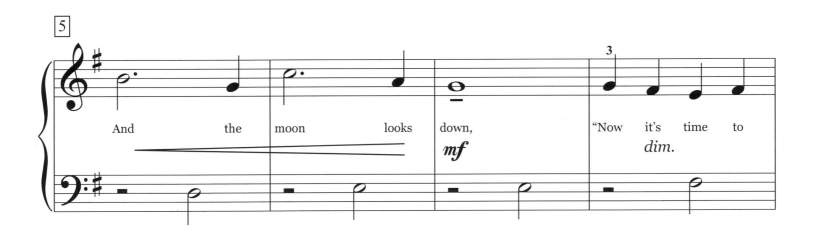

Composer **Naoko Ikeda** grew up and still resides in the beautiful city of Sapporo in northern Japan. Influenced by classical music, jazz, and pop—as well as the piano works of William Gillock—her own compositions reflect her diverse tastes with elegance and humor. Ms. Ikeda is a proud graduate of the Hokusei Gakuen school system and holds a piano performance degree from Yamaguchi College of Arts. She maintains an energetic schedule as both teacher and composer.